Embracing the

Kingdom

A Bible Study on Conversion

A Catholic Bible Study

By Rich Cleveland

Preface

Embracing the Kingdom is the second in a series of Scripture-based discussion books developed for use within Catholic communities. These materials were developed, field-tested, and successfully used through the Small Catholic Communities at Holy Apostles Catholic Church in Colorado Springs, Colorado.

These materials are designed to provide foundational training in both personal spirituality and the ability to participate successfully in a small group. Participants learn to enjoy daily Bible reading and prayer and to make these disciplines a significant resource in their relationship with Christ. Regular meditation on Scripture and meaningful participation in discussion of the Scriptures are developed as other valuable disciplines. These disciplines are nourished in a loving, caring environment that can lead to a motivating, caring Christian community.

These booklets incorporate reflection on Scripture passages around various important topics of personal spirituality and discipleship. Each discussion topic is presented and reinforced by references to valuable Catholic resources.

A leader's guide is available to provide facilitators with resource suggestions for handling the various sessions and creating helpful small-group dynamics. This guide is available as a free download at www.emmausjourney.org.

Acknowledgments

I would like to acknowledge the dedicated help and partnership of my wife Gail in the development of these materials. I am also grateful to Fr. Paul Wicker, pastor of Holy Apostles Catholic Church and the members of the small Catholic communties in this parish—all of whom made the development of these materials possible.

Emmaus Journey is an evangelization and discipleship ministry of
The Navigators, an interdenominational religious organization,
conducted in and through Catholic parishes.

Table of Contents

I would like to recommend for your consideration and use these Emmaus Journey Bible studies. These studies were developed within the Holy Apostles Parish and honor both the value of Scripture reflection and respect for Catholic faith, culture, and tradition.

Go and Make Disciples, published by the National Council of Catholic Bishops, suggests as its first goal: "To bring about in all Catholics such an enthusiasm for their faith that, in living their faith in Jesus, they freely share it with others." These Bible studies were designed for and help accomplish this goal. The following objectives which *Go and Make Disciples* recommends are furthered through these studies:

• "To foster an experience of conversion and renewal in the heart of every believer, leading to a more active living of Catholic life."

• "To foster an appreciation of God's word in the lives of all Catholics."

• "To foster a renewed understanding of the faith among Catholics."

• "To foster a sense of discipleship among Catholic adults."

• "To foster active and personal religious experience through participation in small-group and communal experiences in which the Good News is shared, experienced, and applied to daily life."

The author, Rich Cleveland, has developed the Small Catholic Communities ministry at Holy Apostles Parish for four years. I have experienced our parishioners coming alive in their Catholic faith through these Bible studies. I pray that God will use this to further his life and work in your heart.

Sincerely,
Fr. Paul Wicker, Pastor
Holy Apostles Catholic Church

Session 1

Introduction

▶ **Before You Begin**

Get acquainted with the others in your group by sharing your answers to these questions:
- What is your name?
- How many states or countries have you visited?
- Which one was the most interesting? Why?

Speaking of small groups of Catholic believers meeting like this in community, Pope Paul VI in *Evangelii Nuntiandi* says that they "will be a hope for the universal Church." So, what you are doing by participating in this group is extremely important. Pope Paul VI listed seven characteristics which will enable groups like this to remain valuable and vital as a community and to the Church community at large. They are:

- "That they seek their nourishment in the word of God and do not allow themselves to be ensnared by political polarization or fashionable ideologies."

- "That they avoid the ever present temptation of systematic protest and a hypercritical attitude."

- "That they remain firmly attached to the local Church in which they are inserted, and to the universal Church."

- "That they maintain a sincere communion with the pastors whom the Lord gives to His Church."

- "That they never look on themselves as the sole beneficiaries or sole agents of evangelization—or even the only depositaries of the Gospel."

- "That they grow in missionary consciousness, fervor, commitment and zeal."

- "That they show themselves universal in all things and never sectarian."

These Emmaus Journey materials can help create this environment of hope of which Pope Paul VI speaks. As you apply yourself to these studies, you will find God's word nourishing your spirit. As a result, you'll find your attitudes, words, and behavior and your commitment to the Lord and his people—growing as well.

In *One Heart, One Mind* you began developing the habit of daily reading and meditating on Scripture passages while marking what you read. As you know, this process allows the Holy Spirit to impress various truths on your heart and provides daily encouragement, guidance, and challenge. As you continue in *Embracing the Kingdom,* you will have an opportunity to build on the habits you've previously learned by continuing this process of daily reading, meditating on the Scripture and journaling one or more thoughts. To encourage you to develop this habit further, the first few minutes of each session in *Embracing the Kingdom* will be devoted to sharing from your daily Scripture reading and prayer. Due to space limitations, journal pages are not included in this booklet. Any blank notebook will do, however. Or, you can purchase a prayer journal from The Word Among Us.

Materials

In the *Embracing the Kingdom* studies you will use topical materials—studies based on specific topics—that allow you to explore what different authors have said about a given topic. Though specific passages form the core of the study, the surrounding verses can give you a broader context and additional light on the topic. As you work your way through this Emmaus Journey series, you will also find that the material progresses in terms of both content and difficulty. In these initial sessions we will deal with foundational spiritual issues such as the importance of God's word to our lives. Later sessions build on this foundation and focus on such topics as our responsibility to take the gospel to the world. Consequently, don't be surprised to find yourself growing spiritually as you progress through this material.

Bible Aids

As you work though each session, it is probably a good idea to deal initially with just the Scripture passages listed and the questions in the study. Sit quietly with the word of God and let the Spirit speak to your heart before you read commentaries or other study aids. Give God a chance to speak before you let scholars or commentators add their insights. Then, after you complete the study, feel free to refer to helpful Bible study aids, such as the notes in *The Catholic Study Bible* and the new *Catechism of the Catholic Church*.

Applications

Application questions are designed to be more personal than others. You will never be required to share these answers unless it is helpful to you. However, it is important for your own growth to answer these questions honestly. You may also find it helpful to talk through your new understandings and ideas with others.

Helpful Attitudes

What attitudes help create a successful Bible study?

1. **Preparation.** The Bible study discussion is built on the premise that each person has invested the time to think about the passages and answer the questions. To be unprepared turns the Bible study discussion into a sharing of opinions. Though you may not be able to prepare every time, to choose not to prepare deprives the group of the blessings of God working in your life. Selecting a specific time to do your study each week and establishing a consistent place to study can help you be prepared.

2. **Teachability.** Try to be open to discover new truths and look at old truths in a new way. We always learn more as we open ourselves up to new concepts.

3. **Wholeheartedness.** There may be days when you feel too emotionally and spiritually down to participate in the Bible discussion. While it is helpful to acknowledge these feelings, giving in to them can negatively affect the whole group's experience. God can use the discussion and community experience to lift your spirits. Try to participate enthusiastically even when you don't feel like it.

4. **Willingness to apply what you've learned.** The purpose of Bible study is to change lives, which means changing our attitudes and behavior. The process of bringing new attitudes and behavior to life is stifled when we close ourselves off to the attitude and behavior changes we

feel God is asking of us. On the other hand, when we apply the truths we've discovered in the Scriptures, our lives can change dramatically. These will grow into mature values as you continue to follow Christ.

5. **Respect for all contributions and contributors to the discussion.** Each of the members of your group will approach the study from different backgrounds and different ways of thinking. Each person has a valuable contribution to make. It is important to listen and learn from one another.

Group Conversational Prayer Exercise

One major breakthrough in small Christian communities takes place when the participants discover the power of prayer they possess as a group. Once this power is discovered, the sincerity and faithfulness of the group to pray for one another, both when they are together and when they are apart, increases substantially. Everyone reaches a new level of joy and faith as they see God answer their prayers again and again. They also reach a new level of understanding as to how to pray according to God's will.

Read Acts 12:1-17 together and discover an exciting and somewhat humorous example of what can happen when believers pray as a group. How is your group, and the people praying in this passage, similar or different?

_____

_____

_____

_____

What does this passage teach you about God's power and group prayer?

_____

_____

_____

_____

> Prayer is an all-efficient panoply, a treasure undiminished, a mine never exhausted, a sky unobstructed by clouds, a haven unruffled by storm. It is the root, the fountain and the mother of a thousand blessings. It exceeds a monarch's power....I speak not of the prayer which is cold and feeble and devoid of zeal. I speak of that which proceeds from a mind outstretched, the child of a contrite spirit, the offspring of a soul converted—this is the prayer which mounts to heaven. —St. John Chrysostom, *Ancient Christian Commentary on the Scriptures,* Vol. 2, p. 162

As Catholics we have learned to pray together in many meaningful ways, but we may feel hesitant to pray extemporaneously in a small group. There really is no need to be hesitant or timid! Conversational prayer does not require us to be theologians, only sincere. Those who never experience this freedom to share their heart in prayer in a small group are deprived of a really joyous freedom. In addition, the group is deprived of our contribution as the Holy Spirit speaks through us.

Conversational prayer is simply entering into a group conversation with our heavenly Father. He doesn't care about the polish of our words, only their presence. Here are some simple suggestions that should free you up to pray in the group:

- **Start small.** If you aren't accustomed to praying aloud in a group simply begin by offering a short one-sentence prayer.

- **Pray briefly.** You don't need to offer lengthy prayers. As you become more comfortable hearing your own voice, you can expand your prayer to two or three sentences. It is not in the volume of our request that we are heard but in the sincerity of our request.

- **Pray conversationally.** Don't feel the pressure to pray formally using ecclesiastical, or "churchy", words and phrases. Simply express your thoughts as you would in everyday life.

- **Pray randomly.** Don't feel that you have to start praying just because the person next to you has stopped. Talking in sequence around the circle is not the way a group normally carries on a conversation, and neither should it be the way we pray. Pray when you desire to, or when a subject comes up in prayer that you also want to pray about.

- **Cover one topic at a time.** If someone in the group prays about a topic, someone's health problem for instance, and you also are concerned about that person, that is the time for you also to join in prayer. Then as one subject has been prayed for, someone else can introduce some new prayer concern.

- **Pray from the heart.** The Holy Spirit will take your words and bring them to the Father as they should be. Scripture says: "The Spirit helps us in our weakness; for we do not know how to pray as we ought, but that very Spirit himself intercedes for us with sighs too deep for words. And God, who searches the heart, knows what is the mind of the Spirit, because the Spirit intercedes for the saints according to the will of God" (Romans 8:26-27).

Begin to apply these suggestions as you close this session. Take just a moment to identify concerns people have about which participants of the group would like prayer. Include prayer for this group and for the material you will be covering in the future. Encourage everyone to break the ice and pray briefly.

▶ Preparation for Session 2

1. Continue reading and marking your Bible daily, recording your progress in your spiritual journal.

2. Complete questions 1-4 of the Bible study, "The Importance of God's Word," pages 19-23.

The Importance of God's Word

► **Before You Begin**

Share insights from your daily Bible reading.

The Scriptures always have been esteemed by the Church as critically important to both individual believers and the Christian community. In *The Interpretation of the Bible in the Church*, The Pontifical Biblical Commission says:

It is true that the familiarity with the text of Scripture has been more notable among the faithful at some periods of the church's history than in others. But Scripture has been at the forefront of all important moments of renewal in the life of the church, from the monastic movement of the early centuries to the recent era of the Second Vatican Council. (p. 29)

Catholic leaders in past and recent history have underscored the value of God's word in our lives:

"Ignorance of Scripture is ignorance of Jesus Christ."
—St. Jerome

"A man who is well grounded in the testimonies of the Scripture is the bulwark of the Church."
—St. Jerome

"The call to conversion challenges me to investigate my life plan against the lessons of scripture. I will need to consider reorientation of my values and priorities…in order to make a commitment to Christ, to become a follower of Christ, and to be like Christ."

—Lawrence Boadt, C.S.P. in *The New Catholic Evangelization,* p. 143

It is crucial that we all develop convictions about the importance of God's word. To help develop these deep convictions, study the following Scripture passages.

1.(a) The writer of Psalm 19:7-11 (NAB 8-12) enumerates several benefits we can expect from knowing God's word (referred to as his decrees, statutes, commandments, ordinances, judgments, precepts, and law). Identify as many benefits as you can in this passage, and write them in your own words.

_____

_____

_____

_____

_____

_____

_____

_____

_____

_____

_____

_____

_____

_____

_____

_____

_____

_____

_____

(b) Which of these benefits do you believe is most important? Why?

_____

_____

_____

_____

_____

_____

_____

_____

_____

_____

_____

_____

_____

_____

2.(a) Psalm 119 is not only the longest psalm, but the longest chapter in the Bible. It focuses on the value of a life centered on obedience to God's word. In the passages listed below, what responses to God's word does the psalmist commend?

Psalm 119:2-4

_____

_____

_____

_____

Psalm 119:11-16

_____
_____
_____
_____
_____

Psalm 119:33-34

_____
_____
_____
_____
_____

Psalm 119:97-103

_____
_____
_____
_____
_____

(b) Which of these responses do you feel is most desirable? Why?

_____
_____
_____
_____
_____
_____
_____
_____

3. What additional value does the Scripture have for us, according to 2 Timothy 3:14-17?

_____

_____

_____

_____

_____

_____

_____

_____

_____

_____

_____

_____

_____

_____

Since, therefore, all that the inspired authors, or sacred writers, affirm should be regarded as affirmed by the Holy Spirit, we must acknowledge that the books of Scripture, firmly, faithfully and without error, teach that truth which God, for the sake of our salvation, wished to see confided to the sacred Scriptures. Thus "all Scripture is inspired by God."

—Dogmatic Constitution on Divine Revelation (*Dei Verbum,* 11)

4. What principles for successful living can you discover in Psalm 1:1-3?

_____

_____

_____

_____

_____

_____

_____

_____

_____

_____

_____

_____

_____

_____

_____

▶ **Assignment for Session 3:**

1. Continue reading and marking your Bible daily, recording your progress in your Spiritual Journal.

2. Complete questions 5-8 on "The Importance of God's Word," pages 27-29.

Notes for Session 2

Notes for Session 2

Session 3

The Importance of God's Word (continued)

▶ **Before You Begin**

Share insights from your daily Bible reading.

In the previous session you learned that the Scriptures, when applied to your life, have great value and provide many benefits. How is it possible that the Scriptures provide such life-giving strength and nourishment for our faith?

> For since [the Scriptures] are inspired by God and committed to writing once and for all time, they present God's own word in an unalterable form, and they make the voice of the Holy Spirit sound again and again in the words of the prophets and apostles. It follows that all the preaching of the Church, as indeed the entire Christian religion, should be nourished and ruled by sacred Scripture. In the sacred books the Father who is in heaven comes lovingly to meet his children, and talks with them.
> —*Dogmatic Constitution on Divine Revelation,* 21

This session addresses two questions: 1) How does a person gain nourishment from God's word? 2) What does it mean to be "ruled by sacred Scripture"?

5.(a) Several of these passages refer to the value of meditating on Scriptures. How would you define "meditation on God's word"?

_____

_____

_____

_____

_____

_____

(b) What practical methods for meditating on God's word have you found helpful?

_____

_____

_____

_____

_____

6.(a) From Jesus' example in Matthew 4:1-11, what lessons can we learn about the help of Scripture in overcoming temptation?

_____

_____

_____

_____

_____

(b) From this passage and others you may know, how would you describe Jesus' view of Scripture?

_____

_____

_____

_____

_____

_____

_____

7. Judging from the following passages, what should our rresponse be to Scripture?

Acts 17:11

_____

_____

_____

_____

_____

1 Thessalonians 2:13

_____

_____

_____

_____

_____

James 1:21-25

_____
_____
_____
_____
_____
_____

2 Peter 3:15-18

_____
_____
_____
_____
_____

8. Describe your current convictions regarding Scripture and the role you believe it should have in your life.

_____
_____
_____
_____
_____
_____
_____
_____
_____
_____
_____

Because of limited time, this study does not include a discussion of the value of "sacred tradition" or the "living teaching office" of the Church. A comprehensive explanation of the relationship between Scripture, tradition, and the teaching office of the church can be found in the *Dogmatic Constitution on Divine Revelation* (Dei Verbum) and the new *Catechism of the Catholic Church.*

▶ Assignment for Session 4:

1. Continue reading and marking your Bible daily, recording your progress in your Spiritual Journal.

2. Complete questions 1–3 on "The Importance of Prayer," pages 35-39.

Notes for Session 3

Notes for Session 3

Notes for Session 3

The Importance of Prayer

▶ Before You Begin

Share insights from your daily Bible reading.

Great is the mystery of the faith! . . . This mystery, then, requires that the faithful believe in it, that they celebrate it, and that they live from it in a vital and personal relationship with the living and true God. This relationship is prayer.

So begins the section on "Christian Prayer" in the *Catechism of the Catholic Church* (#2258). The Catechism establishes the vital link between living our faith and prayer. Prayer is a wonderful opportunity—it is the lifeline that makes life in Christ personal and real. Prayer is both a relationship to be experienced and a habit that needs to be encouraged and developed. Yet it can be easy to neglect prayer if we don't recognize its importance, or if we are reluctant to give it the commitment it deserves.

During Jesus' short life and ministry, he frequently taught his disciples about prayer. Equally important, it was the example of his life—so much so that his disciples asked him to teach them to pray (Luke 11:1).

Studying these passages can help you grow in both your understanding and commitment to prayer.

1. (a) What is the privilege we enjoy regarding prayer? (Hebrews 4:14-16)

_____

_____

_____

_____

_____

_____

_____

_____

_____

(b) On what basis can we participate in the privilege of prayer?

_____

_____

_____

_____

_____

_____

_____

_____

_____

2. In Matthew 6:5-15 Jesus teaches his followers about prayer.

(a) In your own words, describe the practices Jesus urged his followers to avoid.

_____

_____

_____

_____

_____

_____

_____

_____

_____

_____

(b) What attitudes about prayer do you think these practices reflect?

_____

_____

_____

_____

_____

_____

_____

_____

_____

(c) Try to identify seven ingredients of the Lord's Prayer by restating
each request in your own words. (verses 9-15)

_____

_____

_____

_____

_____

_____

_____

_____

_____

_____

_____

(d) What patterns or principles of prayer can you discern from the prayer Jesus taught?

_____

_____

_____

_____

_____

_____

_____

_____

_____

_____

> The Lord's Prayer is the most perfect of prayers. . . . In it we ask, not only for all the things we can rightly desire, but also in the sequence that they should be desired. This prayer not only teaches us to ask for things, but also in what order we should desire them. —St. Thomas Aquinas, quoted in *Catechism of the Catholic Church*, 2263

3. Interspersed throughout the Gospels are many other lessons Jesus taught about prayer. What important guidelines, principles, or attitudes about prayer are conveyed in following passages?

Matthew 21:18-22

_____

_____

_____

_____

_____

_____

Luke 11:5-13

_____

_____

_____

_____

_____

John 14:12-14

_____

_____

_____

_____

_____

John 15:7-11

_____

_____

_____

_____

_____

John 16:22-24

_____

_____

_____

_____

_____

_____

▶ **Assignment for Session 5:**

1. Continue reading and marking your Bible daily, recording your progress in your spiritual journal.

2. Complete questions 4-7 on "The Importance of Prayer," pages 43–46.

Notes for Session 4

Notes for Session 4

Notes for Session 4

Notes for Session 4

The Importance of Prayer (continued)

▶ **Before You Begin**

Share insights from your daily Bible reading.

Prayer is such a broad aspect of the Christian life that in these studies we will give it only a brief, practical look. Because of the pressures and demands we often feel, petition and intercession can comprise a major portion of our prayer. As people look at the struggles they face, they realize the need for help beyond their own abilities. So they pray to a loving Father.

In his book, *Life Together*, Dietrich Bonhoeffer states: "A Christian fellowship lives and exists by the intercession of its members for one another, or it collapses. . . Intercession means no more than to bring our brother into the presence of God, to see him under the Cross of Jesus as a poor human being and sinner in need of grace" (p. 86).

Intercession touches the lives of those around us, even those we may consider enemies. Through prayer, we can bring people with us into God's presence. This not only affects the circumstances of their lives, but our relationship with them. Intercession changes things. Jesus knew this, and so he taught his disciples to pray. And his disciples, by word and example, teach us to pray, as you will discover in this study.

4. Why do you think Jesus put such emphasis on encouraging his disciples to pray and to understand prayer?

_____

_____

_____

_____

_____

_____

_____

_____

_____

5. The epistles provide many practical insights on prayer. What do the following passages teach about prayer?
Philippians 4:4-7

_____

_____

_____

_____

_____

1 Timothy 4:4-5

_____

_____

_____

_____

_____

James 4:1-3

_____

_____

_____

_____

_____

_____

James 5:13-18

_____

_____

_____

_____

_____

_____

1 John 5:13-15

_____

_____

_____

_____

_____

A prayer, prayed from the heart, heals. When you know the Our Father, the Apostles' Creed, the "Glory Be to the Father" by heart, you have something to start with. . . . You will be constantly distracted by your worries, but if you keep going back to the words of the prayer, you will gradually discover that your worries become less obsessive and that you really start to enjoy praying. And as the prayer descends from your mind into the center of your being you will discover its healing power. —Henri J.M. Nouwen, *Here and Now,* p. 9

6. Frequently, prayer never gets beyond a concern over problems and difficulties. Yet the prayers we see in the New Testament almost always reflect a broader vision and hope. Read the following passages and write down some of these broader areas that could become the focus of prayer.

Matthew 9:35-38

_____

_____

_____

_____

_____

_____

Ephesians 1:15-23

_____

_____

_____

_____

_____

_____

Ephesians 5:17-20

_____

_____

_____

_____

_____

_____

1 Timothy 2:1-4

_____

_____

_____

_____

_____

_____

7. How have your attitudes, understanding, or feelings about prayer
changed as you've studied these passages?

_____

_____

_____

_____

_____

_____

_____

_____

_____

_____

_____

"God wills that our desire should be exercised in prayer, that we may
be able to receive what he is prepared to give."
—St. Augustine, quoted in the _Catechism of the Catholic Church,_ 2737

▶ Assignment for Session 6:

1. Continue reading and marking your Bible daily, recording
   your progress in your spiritual journal.

2. Complete Questions 1–4 on "The Importance of One
   Another," pages 52-56.

Notes for Session 5

Notes for Session 5

Session 6

The Importance of One Another

▶ **Before You Begin**

Share insights from your daily Bible reading.

As you enter your seventh week of meeting, you may find yourself struggling to remain consistent in daily Bible reading and prayer. Let your focus be renewed by the following words from C.S. Lewis, writing about the importance of training ourselves in the "habit of faith."

> The next step is to make sure that, if you have once accepted Christianity, then some of its main doctrines shall be deliberately held before your mind for some time every day. That is why daily prayers and religious readings and churchgoing are necessary parts of the Christian life. We have to be continually reminded of what we believe. Neither this belief nor any other will automatically remain alive in the mind. It must be fed.
> —*The Inspirational Writings of C.S. Lewis,* p. 337

In the midst of your hectic life, daily Bible reading and prayer enable you to devote a few minutes each day to feeding and nourishing your soul. The goal is to develop intimacy and communication with Christ, thus strengthening and developing your life of faith. The process allows God to speak to you as the Holy Spirit impresses Scripture's truths on your heart. You then can express back to God your love, thanks, and concerns.

C. S. Lewis continues, in the passage quoted above, by explaining how people lose their faith:

> As a matter of fact, if you examined a hundred people who had lost their faith in Christianity, I wonder how many of them would turn out to have been reasoned out of it by honest argument? Do not most people simply drift away?

Daily Bible reading and prayer—along with other spiritual disciplines—function as an anchor, preventing us from simply drifting away from faith. The Christian life is, and should be, a wonderful, dynamic, life-changing, and life-fulfilling relationship with Christ. God allows you to decide whether you develop it or simply let it ebb away. Reaffirm your determination to develop these habits for a lifetime, since they hold such promise.

"Habit is a cable;
we weave a thread of it every day,
and at last we cannot break it."
—Horace Mann

Bible Study

One of the great legacies of Vatican II was the renewed recognition of the place of Jesus Christ—as Savior and Lord—at the center of our Catholic faith. Vatican II emphasized the centrality of the life, death and resurrection of Jesus Christ, his ascension to the Father and his sending of the Holy Spirit. Vatican II helped Catholics see more clearly that belonging to a community of disciples who follow Jesus is more primary than belonging to an institutional church. The Church, rather than being viewed as a structure or institution, is best seen as a community of disciples that carries on Jesus' mission of salvation and healing.
—Frank DeSiano, CSP, and Kenneth Boyack, CSP,
Creating the Evangelizing Parish, P. 10

The Christian life was never intended to be lived in isolation, but rather as part of a community of believers. Temperaments, nature, and culture often encourage people to live an independent, selfish, superficial existence—separate from one another, rather than in an interdependent, gracious, intimate relationship with one another.

In Scripture, Jesus consistently teaches that we are a body of believers—a family with special privileges and responsibilities. This study will help you see the uniqueness of belonging to the family of believers, known as the body of Christ. You also will see the responsibilities we have for one another.

1. (a) Paul, while praying for the Ephesians, describes the elements of this new family relationship (Ephesians 1:17-23). Identify these important elements in your own words.

_____

_____

_____

_____

_____

_____

_____

_____

_____

_____

(b) What is the relationship of the head to the body? How can this analogy be applied spiritually?

_____

_____

_____

_____

_____

_____

_____

_____

_____

_____

2. Several passages discuss the body of Christ and our relationship to one another. What attitudes and behavior help us overcome our natural tendencies toward a selfish existence?

Romans 12:1-8

_____

_____

_____

_____

_____

1 Corinthians 12:12-27

_____

_____

_____

_____

3. In anticipation of his departure into heaven, Jesus was concerned that the disciples know the importance of loving one another. In the following passages, why did Jesus emphasize love?

John 13:33-35

_____

_____

_____

_____

_____

_____

_____

John 15:12-17

_____

_____

_____

_____

_____

_____

4. From the following passages, identify behavior we should avoid as we relate to one another. Explain why you think this behavior is harmful.

Romans 14:13-23

_____

_____

_____

_____

How can these principles be applied to things other than food?

Galatians 5:24--26

What do you think is the basis of competition?

Colossians 3:9-10

What motivates us to be dishonest with one another?

_____

_____

_____

_____

_____

_____

James 4:11-12, 5:9

_____

_____

_____

_____

_____

Can you think of other attitudes and behavior that should be avoided?

_____

_____

_____

_____

_____

No amount of falls will really undo us if we keep on picking ourselves up each time. We shall of course be very muddy and tattered
children by the time we reach home. . . . The only fatal thing is to
lose one's temper and give it up. It is when we notice the dirt that
God is most present in us: it is the very sign of his presence.
The Inspirational Writings of C. S. Lewis, p.296

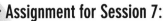 **Assignment for Session 7:**

1. Continue reading and marking your Bible daily, recording `
   your progress in your spiritual journal.

2. Complete questions 5-8 on "The Importance of One
   Another," pages 61-67.

Notes for Session 6

Notes for Session 6

The Importance of One Another (continued)

▶ **Before You Begin**

Share insights from your daily Bible reading.

As people relate to one another, they spend much time trying to avoid saying and doing things prompted by their negative feelings and attitudes. For many people, success means "never having to say you are sorry." But the Christian life is far more than the absence of bad behavior. It is intended to be filled with attitudes and behavior that can only originate from Christ's presence within you.

> All human relationships, be they between parents and children, husbands and wives, lovers and friends, or between members of a community, are meant to be signs of God's love for humanity as a whole and each person in particular. This is a very uncommon viewpoint, but it is the viewpoint of Jesus. Jesus says: 'You must love one another just as I have loved you. It is by your love for one another that everyone will recognize you as my disciples' (John 13:34–35).
> —Henri J.M. Nouwen, *Here and Now,* p. 127

Session 7 focused on attitudes we should avoid when relating with one another. In this session, you'll learn about attitudes and actions Christians should embrace. These bring pleasure and assurance because they reflect that Christ is living *in* you as well as *through* you.

5. What responsibilities do Christians have toward their brothers and sisters in Christ?

Galatians 5:13-14

_____

_____

_____

_____

What do you think makes serving enjoyable?

_____

_____

_____

_____

Ephesians 4:25-29

_____

_____

_____

_____

What motivations should control our speech?

_____

_____

_____

_____

Ephesians 5:21

_____
_____
_____
_____
_____

Why do you think "being in subjection" to another is viewed so negatively?

_____
_____
_____
_____
_____

Colossians 3:12-14

_____
_____
_____
_____
_____

What kind of people need to receive forbearance and forgiveness?

_____
_____
_____
_____
_____

Colossians 3:15-17

_____

_____

_____

_____

_____

Why might people want to avoid this responsibility?

_____

_____

_____

_____

_____

1 Thessalonians 4:18; 5:11

_____

_____

_____

_____

_____

What are some ways to encourage one another?

_____

_____

_____

_____

_____

Hebrews 3:12-14; 10:23-25

_____

_____

_____

_____

_____

What responsibility do you have for helping others remain faithful?

_____

_____

_____

_____

_____

James 5:15–16

_____

_____

_____

_____

Why do you think James lists forgiveness as a kind of condition for a person to receive prayer and support?

_____

_____

_____

_____

_____

6. How do you feel about accepting these responsibilities in your faith community?

_____

_____

_____

_____

_____

_____

_____

_____

_____

_____

_____

_____

7. In dealing with others in the body of Christ, you will inevitably have interpersonal conflict. That's why the Bible provides so much encouragement to forgive and so many guidelines on how to forbear with one another. Two passages provide significant insight on resolving interpersonal conflicts. Compare and contrast the guidelines in Matthew 5:22–24 and Matthew 18:15, 35.

_____

_____

_____

_____

_____

_____

_____

_____

8. What should govern our forgiveness of others when they wrong us?

Colossians 3:13

_____

_____

_____

_____

We are to forgive others as God has forgiven us. How would you characterize God's forgiveness in the following passages?

Jeremiah 31:34

_____

_____

_____

_____

Ephesians 1:7-8

_____

_____

_____

_____

Colossians 2:13-15

_____

_____

_____

1 John 1:9

_____

_____

_____

_____

_____

In the Western world, the suffering that seems to be the most painful is that of feeling rejected, ignored, despised and left alone. We human beings can suffer immense deprivations with great steadfastness, but when we sense that we no longer have anything to offer anyone, we quickly lose our grip on life. Instinctively we know that the joy of life comes from the ways in which we live together and that the pain in life comes from the many ways that we fail to do that well. —Henri J. M. Nouwen, *Life of the Beloved*

▶ **Assignment for Session 8:**

1. Continue reading and marking your Bible daily, recording your progress in your spiritual journal.

2. Complete questions 1–5 on "The Importance of Conversion," pages 75-78.

Notes for Session 7

Notes for Session 7

Notes for Session 7

Notes for Session 7

The Importance of Conversion

▶ **Before You Begin**

Share insights from your daily Bible reading

Paul tells us in 2 Corinthians 5:17: "If anyone is in Christ, there is a new creation: everything old has passed away; see, everything has become new!"

Conversion is the foundation and wellspring of spiritual transformation. God uses this transformation—brought about by the Holy Spirit within us—to permeate and affect everything in our lives. The transformation brought about by conversion is both immediate and continual, and without it, we really don't experience new life.

> "Conversion is the change of our lives that comes about through the power of the Holy Spirit. All who accept the Gospel undergo change as we continually put on the mind of Christ by rejecting sin and becoming more faithful disciples in his Church. Unless we undergo conversion, we have not truly accepted the Gospel."
> —*Go and Make Disciples: A National Plan and Strategy for Catholic Evangelization*, p. 2

Hopefully, you will experience many moments of conversion during your lifetime, moments when the Holy Spirit gives you the understanding, desire, and power to bring a deeper level of commitment to your life. In the next two studies, you will learn about three important responses of commitment: faith, obedience, and service.

"This is crucial: We must be converted—and we must continue to be converted! We must let the Holy Spirit change our lives!
—*Go and Make Disciples: A National Plan and Strategy for Catholic Evangelization*, p. 2

1. Nicodemus' life-changing encounter with Christ is recorded in John 3:1–21. What primary issues did Jesus stress during this encounter?

_____

_____

_____

_____

_____

_____

_____

_____

_____

Write in your own words the promise(s) Jesus shared with Nicodemus.

_____

_____

_____

_____

_____

_____

_____

_____

_____

What conditions does Jesus put on obtaining these promises?

_____

_____

_____

_____

_____

_____

_____

_____

2. Using Paul's explanation in Ephesians 2:1–10, make a list of the essential ingredients of the gospel.

_____

_____

_____

_____

_____

_____

_____

_____

_____

_____

_____

_____

_____

_____

_____

_____

_____

3. As Catholics, we should not shy away from phrases like "born again," "by grace," and "through faith," which we have found in the above passages, for they are a part of *our* Bible and *our* faith. Read the following statement from *Go and Make Disciples* and circle those phrases which correspond to these terms.

Our message of faith proclaims an eternally faithful God, creating all in love and sustaining all with gracious care. We proclaim that God, whose love is unconditional, offers us divine life even in the face of our sin, failures, and inadequacies. We believe in a God who became one of us in Jesus, God's Son, whose death and resurrection bring us salvation. We believe that the risen Christ sends his own Spirit upon us when we respond to him in faith and repentance, making us his people, the Church, and giving us the power of new life and guiding us to our eternal destiny (p. 3).

4. When an infant is baptized, it is done on the basis of the faith of his or her parents. But at some point in life, each of us needs to make our own decisions, affirming our faith in Jesus. How would you describe your journey in this adult faith decision to "respond to him in faith and repentance"?

_____

_____

_____

_____

_____

_____

_____

_____

_____

_____

_____

_____

_____

_____

_____

_____

_____

_____

5. God doesn't want us to be fearful or apprehensive about our fate. That's why he's given us both his word and his Spirit as anchors for our lives. What "anchors" can you find in 1 John 5:9-15?

_____

_____

_____

_____

_____

_____

_____

_____

_____

_____

_____

_____

_____

_____

_____

Believing in Jesus Christ and in the One who sent him for our salvation is necessary for obtaining that salvation. Since 'without faith it is impossible to please [God]' and to attain to the fellowship of his sons, therefore without faith no one has ever attained justification, nor will anyone obtain eternal life "but he who endures to the end." —*Catechism of the Catholic Church,* 161

▶ Assignment for Session 9:

1. Continue reading and marking your Bible daily, recording your progress in your spiritual journal.

2. Complete questions 6-11 on "The Importance of Conversion," pages 81-85.

Notes for Session 8

Notes for Session 8

Notes for Session 8

Notes for Session 8

The Importance of Conversion (continued)

▶ **Before You Begin**

Share insights from your daily Bible reading.

People use various terms—"born again," "saved," "accept Christ," and "receive Christ"— to describe the response of faith we studied in the last session. These terms all refer to a personal response that signifies, in the words of *Go and Make Disciples*, a person's belief in these truths:

- •"God, whose love is unconditional,

- offers us divine life even in the face of our sin, failures, and inadequacies. . . .

- He became one of us in Jesus, God's Son,

- whose death and resurrection bring us salvation. . . .

- Christ sends his own Spirit upon us when we respond to him in faith and repentance,

- making us his people, the Church,

- and giving us the power of new life and guiding us to our eternal destiny."

Both Peter and Paul refer to this initial event of faith as the first step of obedience (Romans 1:5, 1 Peter 1:2) in a lifestyle of obedience to Jesus. Because of human abuses of authority, people often have an aversion to the concept of obedience. But for the Christian, a life of obedience is a joy. Obedience is a key way in which we can express our faith in and love for God.

6. As Jesus was preparing to go to the cross, he spent his last hours with his disciples discussing the importance of obedience (John 14:15-24). What does Jesus say is the motivation for responding to him in obedience?

_____

_____

_____

_____

_____

_____

_____

_____

_____

_____

_____

_____

What provisions does Jesus give to help us live a life of obedience?

_____

_____

_____

_____

_____

_____

_____
_____
_____
_____
_____
_____
_____
_____

7. Romans 12:1-2 and Ephesians 4:20-24 explain several elements we need to respond to Christ in obedience. Identify these elements and write them in your own words.

_____
_____
_____
_____
_____
_____
_____
_____
_____
_____
_____
_____
_____
_____

8. Paul continues in Ephesians 4:25–5:14 by listing several behavioral changes that reflect a life of obedience. Which three changes do you believe are most important? Why?

_____

_____

_____

_____

_____

_____

_____

_____

_____

_____

_____

_____

By faith, man completely submits his intellect and his will to God. With his whole being man gives his assent to God the revealer. Sacred Scripture calls this human response to God, the author of revelation, "the obedience of faith."
—*Catechism of the Catholic Church,* 143

As we respond to Jesus in faith and obedience, our love for him will naturally be expressed in a desire to serve him. Our joy and appreciation for all that he does for us causes us to share Jesus through our words, actions, and attitudes. Through these next questions, let's examine the privilege Christ offers of responding in service.

9. Why has God given us individual gifts, abilities, and talents?
1 Corinthians 12:4-7,25

_____

_____

_____

_____

_____

_____

What are some of the gifts, abilities, and talents God has given you?

_____

_____

_____

_____

_____

_____

How do you think you can use one or more of these talents to serve him?

_____

_____

_____

_____

_____

_____

10. What principles for serving do you find in 1 Peter 4:7-11?

_____

_____

_____

_____

_____

_____

_____

_____

_____

_____

_____

_____

11. What additional motivation do you find in Mark 10:41-45 for making a committed response to serve?

_____

_____

_____

_____

_____

"Discipleship means following Jesus as a way of life along with others who have chosen to follow him, using one's gifts and skills in service to the community and the world. The qualities of discipleship, clearly shown throughout the New Testament, include: a readiness to respond, an ability to participate and learn, a generous giving of oneself, an attitude free from self-centeredness, and a desire to go further on the journey." —Frank DeSiano, C.S.P., and Kenneth Boyack, C.S.P., in *Creating the Evangelizing Parish,* p. 139

▶ Assignment for Session 10:

1. Continue reading and marking your Bible daily, recording your progress in your Spiritual Journal.

2. Complete questions 1-7 on "The Importance of Faith," pages 91-94.

Notes for Session 9

Notes for Session 9

Notes for Session 9

The Importance of Faith

▶ **Before You Begin**

Share insights from your daily Bible reading.

P lease allow me to shout it aloud: 'It is time to return to God!' The person who does not yet have the joy of faith is asked for the courage to seek it with confidence, perseverance and openness. Whoever has the grace of possessing it is asked to value it as the most treasured possession of his life, living it thoroughly and witnessing to it with passion. Our world hungers for faith, for an authentic and deep faith, because God alone can fully satisfy the desires of the human heart."
—John Paul II, from "It Is Time to Return to God!" *L'Osservatore Romano* as quoted in *The Catholic Church at the End of an Age,* by Ralph Martin (p. 233)

Faith opens our lives to the working of the Holy Spirit and enables us to appropriate more fully God's grace on a daily basis. As Pope John II said, "valuing it, living it, and witnessing to it makes relationships with Jesus come alive. The more we share our faith, the more it multiplies."

The Book of Romans includes an extensive explanation of faith. Many of us were baptized as Christians and into the Catholic Church because of our parents' faith. But at some point, each of us needs to reaffirm for ourselves and others that we have embraced faith in Christ as a decision we have freely made. The following passages describe this initial expression of faith.

To be human, "man's response to God by faith must be free, and . . . therefore nobody is to be forced to embrace the faith against his will. The act of faith is of its very nature a free act." "God calls men to serve him in spirit and in truth. Consequently they are bound to him in conscience, but not coerced . . . . This fact received its fullest manifestation in Christ Jesus." Indeed, Christ invited people to faith and conversion, but never coerced them. "For he bore witness to the truth but refused to use force to impose it on those who spoke against it. His kingdom . . . . grows by the love with which Christ, lifted up on the cross, draws men to himself."
—*Catechism of the Catholic Church,* 160

1. How are "embracing the faith" and its effects described in Romans 4:23–5:2?

_____

_____

_____

_____

_____

_____

_____

_____

2. What does Romans 9:30–10:4 describe as an impediment to embracing Christ in an act of faith?

_____

_____

_____

_____

_____

_____

_____

3. Often people make this initial act of faith more complex than God intended. In Romans 10:8–13, Paul offers a simple explanation of what is involved. From this passage, describe how you would help someone express and affirm their faith in Christ.

_____

_____

_____

_____

_____

_____

> Believing in Jesus Christ and in the one who sent him for our salvation is necessary for obtaining that salvation. "Since 'without faith it is impossible to please [God]' and to attain to the fellowship of his sons, therefore without faith no one has ever attained justification, nor will anyone obtain eternal life but he who endures to the end." —*Catechism of the Catholic Church,* 161

If genuinely present in a believer, faith expresses itself in what the New Testament calls "good works." Confusion about the relationship of faith and works often leads to emphasizing one and excluding the other. Yet God ordained that both are vital to our lives as Christians.

4. How does Paul explain the relationship between faith and works in Ephesians 2:4-10?

_____

_____

_____

_____

_____

_____

_____

5. James elaborates on the relationship between faith and works in James 2:14-26. What points does James make about faith and works?

_____

_____

_____

_____

_____

_____

6. How would you define "good works"?

_____

_____

_____

_____

_____

_____

Faith is an entirely free gift that God makes to man. We can lose this priceless gift, as St. Paul indicated to St. Timothy: "Wage the good warfare, holding faith and a good conscience. By rejecting conscience, certain persons have made shipwreck of their faith." To live, grow, and persevere in the faith until the end we must nourish it

with the word of God; we must beg the Lord to increase our faith;
it must be "working through charity," abounding in hope, and
rooted in the faith of the Church.
—*Catechism of the Catholic Church,* 162

7. What can you personally apply to your life from this study on
faith?

_____

_____

_____

_____

_____

_____

_____

_____

_____

▶ **Assignment for Session 11:**

1. Continue reading and marking your Bible daily, recording
   your progress in your spiritual journal.

2. Complete questions 8-12 on "The Importance of Faith,"
   pages 99-101.

Notes for Session 10

Notes for Session 10

Notes for Session 10

Session 11

The Importance of Faith (continued)

▶ **Before You Begin**

Share insights from your daily Bible reading.

In faith, the human intellect and will cooperate with divine grace: "Believing is an act of the intellect assenting to the divine truth by command of the will moved by God through grace. "
—*Catechism of the Catholic Church,* 155

Jesus often spoke about the importance of having faith. He refers to some as, "Ye of little faith" (Matthew 8:26). He commends others, in some cases non-Israelites, for their "great faith" (Luke 7:9). He frequently chides his followers with the question, "Where is your faith?" (5:25). His disciples in turn implore him: "Increase our faith" (17:5)

Where does faith come from? How is it developed? How is it expressed? This session will attempt to answer these questions.

8. Hebrews 11 is a classic, definitive explanation of faith. In verses 4-31, faith is illustrated through the lives of a number of people. Record below six different ways faith was expressed through the lives of these people. Indicate which of these expressions of faith you found most challenging.

_____

_____

_____

_____

_____

_____

_____

_____

_____

_____

9. Hebrews 11:32-40 lists an assortment of accomplishments brought about by faith. What impressed you about faith from this passage?

_____

_____

_____

_____

_____

_____

_____

_____

_____

10. Which model of faith in Hebrews 11 do you find most beneficial for your life? Why?

_____

_____

_____

_____

_____

_____

_____

_____

11. After investing considerable time studying this chapter, how would you elaborate on the explanation of faith given in Hebrews 11:1?

_____

_____

_____

_____

_____

_____

_____

_____

12. This chapter on faith is sandwiched between Hebrews 10:38-39 and Hebrews 12:1-2. These verses point to how we should respond to this chapter on faith and apply it to our lives. In your own words, explain how you think Hebrews 11 should affect your life.

_____

_____

_____

_____

_____

_____

_____

_____

_____

Pope John Paul II has re–echoed Pope Paul's emphasis on evangelization in his statement on catechesis. . . . He also expressed a concern that those engaged in religious education—namely, children, youth, and families—may not be fully benefiting from catechesis because they have not yet heard an effective proclamation of Jesus and the good news. Without such a basic encounter with the Gospel, the impact of catechesis remains limited.

—*Catholic Evangelization Today: A New Pentecost for the United States,* edited by Kenneth Boyack C.S.P. (page 1)

Summary

During these past few months, you have tasted the enjoyment of participating in a Catholic small group. You practiced several new skills for developing your relationship with Christ and deepening your daily participation in Scripture reading and prayer. In addition, you have prepared for and discussed ten studies on:

• The Importance of God's Word
• The Importance of Prayer
• The Importance of One Another
• The Importance of Conversion
• The Importance of Faith

After thinking about your experience during these past few months, write a brief paragraph or two explaining how you feel about your involvement.

_____

_____

_____

_____

_____

_____

_____

_____

_____

You have worked hard, given of yourself, and been open to God's involvement in your life. And this hard work has not gone unrewarded, we are sure! May God continue to reward you as you draw closer to him in his word.

Notes for Session 11

Notes for Session 11

Notes for Session 11

Notes for Session 11

Stop by and see us as you journey on the Web

The Emmaus Journey Catholic Small Group Ministry exists to assist Catholics to grow in their understanding and commitment to God's word.

On the Emmaus Journey web page, small group studies are *free* to download and reproduce for use in your parish. You will find additional small group resources and free downloads to assist you in your small group ministry.

In addition, at *The Word Among Us* web page, we offer *free of charge* –
- the Scripture readings used at Mass for each day
- daily meditations and reflections based on the Mass readings
- practical articles on Christian living
- reviews of the newest Emmaus Journey Bible Studies

Please visit our websites today!

Emmaus Journey
www.emmausjourney.org
email: info@emmausjourney.org
phone: 719-599-0448

the WORD among us
www.wordamongus.org
email: theresa@wau.org
phone: 800-775-9673